CONGREGATION FOR CATHOLIC EDUCATION
(of Seminaries and Educational Institutions)

EDUCATING TOGETHER IN CATHOLIC SCHOOLS

A SHARED MISSION BETWEEN CONSECRATED PERSONS AND THE LAY FAITHFUL

All booklets are published thanks to the generous support of the members of the Catholic Truth Society

CATHOLIC TRUTH SOCIETY
PUBLISHERS TO THE HOLY SEE

Contents

Introduction

1. The unexpected and often contradictory evolution of our age gives rise to educational challenges that pose questions for the school world. They force us to seek appropriate answers not only as regards contents and didactic methods, but also as regards the *community experience* that is a mark of educational activity. The relevance of these challenges transpires from the context of the social, cultural and religious complexity in which young people are actually growing up, and significantly influences their way of living. They are widespread phenomena such as lack of interest for the fundamental truths of human life, individualism, moral relativism and utilitarianism, that permeate above all rich and developed societies. Add to that rapid structural changes, globalisation and the application of new technologies in the field of information that increasingly affect daily life and the process of formation. Moreover, with the process of development, the gap between rich and poor countries grows and the phenomenon of migration increases, so emphasising the diversity of cultural identities in the same territory with the relative consequences concerning integration. In a society that is at once global and diversified, local and planetary, that hosts various and contrasting ways of interpreting the world and life, young people find themselves faced with different proposals of values, or lack thereof, that are increasingly stimulating but also increasingly less shared. There are also the difficulties that arise from problems of family stability, situations of hardship and poverty, that create a widespread feeling of disorientation at the existential and emotional level in a delicate period of their growth and maturation, exposing them to the danger of being "tossed to and fro and carried about with every wind of doctrine" (*Ep* 4:14).

2. In this context it becomes especially urgent to offer young people a course of scholastic formation which is not reduced to a simple individualistic and instrumental fruition of service with a view to obtaining a qualification. As well as gaining knowledge, students must also have a strong experience of sharing with their educators. For this experience to be happily accomplished, educators must

3

be welcoming and well-prepared interlocutors, able to awaken and direct the best energies of students towards the search for truth and the meaning of existence, a positive construction of themselves and of life in view of an overall formation. In the end, "real education is not possible without the light of truth".[1]

3. This perspective regards all scholastic institutions, but even more directly the Catholic school, which is constantly concerned with the formational requirements of society, because "the problem of instruction has always been closely linked to the Church's mission".[2] The Catholic school participates in this mission like a true ecclesial subject, with its educational service that is enlivened by the truth of the Gospel. In fact, faithful to its vocation, it appears "as a place of integral education of the human person through a clear educational project of which Christ is the foundation",[3] directed at creating a synthesis between faith, culture and life.

4. The project of the Catholic school is convincing only if carried out by people who are deeply motivated, because they witness to a living encounter with Christ, in whom alone "the mystery of man truly becomes clear".[4] These persons, therefore, acknowledge a *personal and communal adherence* with the Lord, assumed as the basis and constant reference of the inter-personal relationship and mutual cooperation between educator and student.

5. The implementation of a real *educational community*, built on the foundation of shared projected values, represents a serious task that must be carried out by the Catholic school. In this setting, the presence both of students and of teachers from different cultural and religious backgrounds requires an increased commitment of discernment and accompaniment. The preparation of a shared project acts as a stimulus that should force the Catholic school to

---

[1] Benedict XVI, Address to Rome's Ecclesial Diocesan Convention on the Family and Christian Community (6th June 2005): *AAS* 97 (2005), 816.

[2] John Paul II, Speech to UNESCO (2nd June 1980), n. 18: *AAS* 72 (1980), 747.

[3] Congregation for Catholic Education, *The Catholic School on the Threshold of the Third Millennium* (28th December 1997), n. 4.

[4] Vatican Council II, Pastoral Constitution on the Church in the Modern World *Gaudium et spes* (7th December 1965), no. 22: *AAS* 58 (1966), 1042.

4

be a place of ecclesial experience. Its binding force and potential for relationships derive from a set of values and a *communion of life* that is rooted in our common belonging to Christ. Derived from the recognition of evangelical values are educational norms, motivational drives and also the final goals of the school. Certainly the degree of participation can differ in relation to one's personal history, but this requires that educators be willing to offer a permanent commitment to formation and self-formation regarding a choice of cultural and life values to be made present in the educational community.[5]

6. Having already dealt in two previous separate documents with the themes of the identity and mission of Catholic lay persons and of consecrated persons in schools respectively, this document of the Congregation for Catholic Education considers the pastoral aspects regarding cooperation between lay and consecrated persons[6] within the same educational mission. In it, the choice of the lay faithful to live their educational commitment as "a personal vocation in the Church, and not simply as [...] the exercise of a profession"[7] meets with the choice of consecrated persons, inasmuch as they are called "to live the evangelical councils and bring the humanism of the beatitudes to the field of education and schools".[8]

7. This document constantly refers to previous texts of the Congregation for Catholic Education regarding education and schools[9] and clearly considers the different situations encountered by Catholic Institutions in various parts of the world. It wishes to

---

[5] Cf. Sacred Congregation for Catholic Education, *The Catholic School* (19th March 1977), no. 32.

[6] In this document reference is made to the priests, men and women religious and persons who, with different forms of consecration, choose the path of following Christ to wholeheartedly devote themselves to him (Cf. John Paul II, Post-synodal Apostolic Exhortation *Vita consecrata* (25th March 1996), nos. 1-12: *AAS* 88 (1996), 377-385.

[7] Sacred Congregation for Catholic Education, *Lay Catholics in Schools: Witnesses to Faith* (15th October 1982), no 37.

[8] Congregation for Catholic Education, *Consecrated Persons and their Mission in Schools*, no. 6; Cf. John Paul II, Post-synodal Apostolic Exhortation *Vita consecrata*, no. 96: *AAS* 88 (1996), 471-472.

[9] *The Catholic School* (19th March 1977); *Lay Catholics in Schools: Witnesses to Faith* (15th October 1982); *Educational Guidance in Human Love. Outlines for Sex Education* (1st November 1983); *The Religious Dimension of Education in a Catholic School* (7th April 1988); *The Catholic School on the Threshold of the Third Millennium* (28th December 1997); *Consecrated Persons and their Mission in Schools. Reflections and Guidelines* (28th October 2002).

call attention to three fundamental aspects of cooperation between lay faithful and consecrated persons in the Catholic school: communion in the educational mission, the necessary course of formation for communion for a shared educational mission and, lastly, openness towards others as the fruit of that communion.

I. COMMUNION IN THE MISSION OF EDUCATION

8. Every human being is called to communion because of his nature which is created in the image and likeness of God (cf. *Gn* 1:26-27). Therefore, within the sphere of biblical anthropology, man is not an isolated individual, but a *person*: a being who is essentially relational. The communion to which man is called always involves a double dimension, that is to say vertical (communion with God) and horizontal (communion with people). It is fundamental that communion be acknowledged as a gift of God, as the fruit of the divine initiative fulfilled in the Easter mystery.[10]

The Church: mystery of communion and mission

9. God's original plan was compromised by the sin that wounded all relations: between man and God, between man and man. However, God did not abandon man in solitude, and, in the fullness of time, sent his Son, Jesus Christ, as Saviour,[11] so that man might find, in the Spirit, full communion with the Father. In its turn, communion with the Trinity rendered possible by the encounter with Christ, unites persons with one another.

10. When Christians say communion, they refer to the eternal mystery, revealed in Christ, of the communion of love that is the very life of God-Trinity. At the same time we also say that Christians share in this communion in the Body of Christ which is the Church (cf. *Ph* 1:7; *Rv* 1:9). Communion is, therefore, the "essence" of the Church, the foundation and source of its mission of being in the world "the home and the school of communion",[12] to lead all men and women to enter ever more profoundly into the mystery of Trinitarian communion and, at the same time, to extend and strengthen internal relations within the human community. In this sense, "the Church is like a

---

[10] Cf. Congregation for the Doctrine of the Faith, Letter to the Bishops of the Catholic Church *Communionis Notio*, (28th May 1992), no. 3b: *AAS* 85 (1993), 836.

[11] Cf. Roman missal, Eucharistic prayer IV.

[12] John Paul II, Apostolic Letter *Novo millennio ineunte* (6th January 2001), no. 43: *AAS* 93 (2001), 297.

human family, but at the same time it is also the great family of God, through which he creates a place of communion and unity through all continents, cultures and nations".[13]

11. As a result, therefore, in the Church, which is the *icon of the love incarnate of God*, "communion and mission are profoundly connected with each other, they interpenetrate and mutually imply each other, to the point that communion represents both the source and the fruit of mission: communion gives rise to mission and mission is accomplished in communion".[14]

Educating in communion and for communion

12. Because its aim is to make man more man, education can be carried out authentically only in a relational and community context. It is not by chance that the first and original educational environment is that of the natural community of the family.[15] Schools, in their turn, take their place beside the family as an educational space that is communitarian, organic and intentional and they sustain their educational commitment, according to a logic of assistance.

13. The Catholic school, characterised mainly as an educating community, is a school for the *person and of persons*. In fact, it aims at forming the *person in the integral unity of his being*, using the tools of teaching and learning where "criteria of judgement, determining values, points of interest, lines of thought, sources of inspiration and models of life"[16] are formed. Above all, they are involved in the dynamics of interpersonal relations that form and vivify the school community.

14. On the other hand, because of its identity and its ecclesial roots, this community must aspire to becoming a Christian community,

---

[13] Benedict XVI, Homily at the Prayer Vigil in Marienfeld (20th August 2005): *AAS* 97 (2005), 886.

[14] John Paul II, Post-synodal Apostolic Exhortation *Christifideles laici* (30th December 1988), no. 32: *AAS* 81 (1989), 451-452.

[15] Cf. Vatican Council II, Declaration on Christian Education *Gravissimum educationis* (28th October 1965), no. 3: *AAS* 58 (1966), 731; C.I.C., cann. 793 and 1136.

[16] Paul VI, Post-synodal Apostolic Exhortation *Evangelii nuntiandi* (8th December 1975), no. 19: *AAS* 68 (1976), 18.

that is, a community of faith, able to create increasingly more profound relations of communion which are themselves educational. It is precisely the presence and life of an educational community, in which all the members participate in a fraternal communion, nourished by a living relationship with Christ and with the Church, that makes the Catholic school the environment for an authentically ecclesial experience.

Consecrated persons and the lay faithful together in schools

15. "In recent years, one of the fruits of the teaching on the Church as communion has been the growing awareness that her members can and must unite their efforts, with a view to cooperation and exchange of gifts, in order to participate more effectively in the Church's mission. This helps to give a clearer and more complete picture of the Church herself, while rendering more effective the response to the great challenges of our time, thanks to the combined contributions of the various gifts".[17] In this ecclesial context the mission of the Catholic school, lived as a community formed of consecrated persons and lay faithful, assumes a very special meaning and demonstrates a wealth that should be acknowledged and developed. This mission demands, from all the members of the educational community, the awareness that educators, as persons and as a community, have an unavoidable responsibility to create an original Christian style. They are required to be witnesses of Jesus Christ and to demonstrate Christian life as bearing light and meaning for everyone. Just as a consecrated person is called to testify his or her specific vocation to a life of communion in love[18] so as to be in the scholastic community a sign, a memorial and a prophecy of the values of the Gospel,[19] so too a lay educator is required to exercise "a specific mission within the Church by living,

---

[17] John Paul II, Post-synodal Apostolic Exhortation *Vita consecrata,* n. 54: *AAS* 88 (1996), 426-427. For cooperation between lay faithful and consecrated persons see also nos. 54-56: *AAS* 88 (1996), 426-429.

[18] Cf. Congregation for the Institutes of Consecrated Life and the Societies of Apostolic Life, *Starting Afresh from Christ* (14th June 2002), no. 28.

[19] Cf. Congregation for Catholic Education, *Consecrated Persons and their Mission in Schools,* no. 20.

in faith, a secular vocation in the communitarian structure of the school".[20]

16. What makes this testimony really effective is the promotion, especially within the educational community of the Catholic school, of that *spirituality of communion* that has been indicated as the great prospect awaiting the Church of the Third Millennium. Spirituality of communion means "an ability to think of our brothers and sisters in the faith within the profound unity of the Mystical Body, and therefore as "those who are a part of me",[21] and "the Christian community's ability to make room for all the gifts of the Spirit"[22] in a relationship of reciprocity between the various ecclesial vocations. Even in that special expression of the Church that is the Catholic school, spirituality of communion must become the living breath of the educational community, the criterion for the full ecclesial development of its members and the fundamental point of reference for the implementation of a truly shared mission.

17. This spirituality of communion, therefore, must be transformed into an attitude of clear evangelical fraternity among those persons who profess charisms in Institutes of consecrated life, in movements or new communities, and in other faithful who operate in the Catholic school. This spirituality of communion holds true for the Catholic school, founded by Religious families, by dioceses, by parishes or by the lay faithful, which today takes into itself the presence of ecclesial movements. In this way, the educational community makes room for the gifts of the Spirit and acknowledges these diversities as wealth. A genuine ecclesial maturity, nourished by the encounter with Christ in the sacraments, will make it possible to develop "whether of the more traditional kind or the newer ecclesial movements [...] a vitality that is God's gift",[23] for the entire scholastic community and for the educational journey itself.

---

[20] Sacred Congregation for Catholic Education, *Lay Catholics in Schools: Witnesses to Faith,* no. 24.

[21] John Paul II, Apostolic Letter *Novo millennio ineunte,* no. 43: *AAS* 93 (2001), 297.

[22] *Ibid.,* no. 46: 299.

[23] *Ibid.,* no. 46: 300.

10

18. The Catholic professional associations form another situation of "communion", a structured aid for the educational mission. They are a space for dialogue between families, the local institutions and the school. These associations, with their break-down at local, national and international levels, are a wealth that brings an especially fruitful contribution to the world of education as regards both motivations and professional points of view. Many associations have among their members teachers and persons in responsible positions both from the Catholic school and from other educational situations. Thanks to the pluralism of their origins, they can carry out an important function of dialogue and cooperation between institutions that differ but which have in common the same educational goals. These associative realities are required to consider how situations change, so adapting their structure and their way of operating in order to continue to be an effective and incisive presence in the sector of education. They must also intensify their reciprocal cooperation, especially in order to guarantee the achievement of their common goals, fully respecting the value and specificity of each association.

19. It is, moreover, of fundamental importance that the service carried out by the associations is stimulated by full participation in the pastoral activity of the Church. The Episcopal Conferences and their continental versions are entrusted with the role of promoting the development of the specificities of each association, favouring and encouraging more coordinated work in the educational sector.

II. A JOURNEY OF FORMATION FOR EDUCATING TOGETHER

20. Educating the young generations in communion and for communion in the Catholic school is a serious commitment that must not be taken lightly. It must be duly prepared and sustained through an initial and permanent project of formation that is able to grasp the educational challenges of the present time and to provide the most effective tools for dealing with them within the sphere of a shared mission. This implies that educators must be willing to learn and develop knowledge and be open to the renewal and updating of methodologies, but open also to spiritual and religious formation and sharing. In the context of the present day, this is essential for responding to the expectations that come from a constantly and rapidly changing world in which it is increasingly difficult to educate.

Professional formation

21. One of the fundamental requirements for an educator in a Catholic school is his or her possession of a solid professional formation. Poor quality teaching, due to insufficient professional preparation or inadequate pedagogical methods, unavoidably undermines the effectiveness of the overall formation of the student and of the cultural witness that the educator must offer.

22. The professional formation of the educator implies a vast range of cultural, psychological and pedagogical skills, characterised by autonomy, planning and evaluation capacity, creativity, openness to innovation, aptitude for updating, research and experimentation. It also demands the ability to synthesise professional skills with educational motivations, giving particular attention to the relational situation required today by the increasingly collegial exercise of the teaching profession. Moreover, in the eyes and expectations of students and their families, the educator is seen and desired as a welcoming and prepared interlocutor, able to motivate the young to a complete formation, to encourage and direct their greatest energy and skills towards a positive construction of themselves and their

lives, and to be a serious and credible witness of the responsibility and hope which the school owes to society.

23. The continuous rapid transformation that affects man and today's society in all fields leads to the precocious aging of acquired knowledge that demands new attitudes and methods. The educator is required to constantly update the contents of the subjects he teaches and the pedagogical methods he uses. The educator's vocation demands a ready and constant ability for renewal and adaptation. It is not, therefore, sufficient to achieve solely an initial good level of preparation; rather what is required is to maintain it and elevate it in a journey of permanent formation. Because of the variety of aspects that it involves, permanent formation demands a constant personal and communal search for its forms of achievement, as well as a formation course that is also shared and developed through exchange and comparison between consecrated and lay educators of the Catholic school.

24. It is not sufficient simply to care about professional updating in the strict sense. The synthesis between faith, culture and life that educators of the Catholic school are called to achieve is, in fact, reached "by integrating all the different aspects of human knowledge through the subjects taught, in the light of the Gospel [… and] in the growth of the virtues characteristic of the Christian".[24]

This means that Catholic educators must attain a special sensitivity with regard to the person to be educated in order to grasp not only the request for growth in knowledge and skills, but also the need for growth in humanity. Thus educators must dedicate themselves "to others with heartfelt concern, enabling them to experience the richness of their humanity".[25]

25. For this reason, Catholic educators need "a 'formation of the heart': they need to be led to that encounter with God in Christ which awakens their love and opens their spirits to others", so that their educational commitment becomes "a consequence deriving from their faith, a faith which becomes active through love (cf. *Ga*

---

[24] Sacred Congregation for Catholic Education, *The Catholic School*, no. 37.

[25] Benedict XVI, Encyclical Letter *Deus caritas est* (25th December 2005), no. 31: *AAS* 98 (2006), 244.

5:6)".[26] In fact, even "care for instruction means loving" (*Ws* 6:17). It is only in this way that they can make their teaching a school of faith, that is to say, a transmission of the Gospel, as required by the educational project of the Catholic school.

Theological and spiritual formation

26. The transmission of the Christian message through teaching implies a mastery of the knowledge of the truths of the faith and of the principles of spiritual life that require constant improvement. This is why both consecrated and lay educators of the Catholic school need to follow an opportune formational theological itinerary.[27] Such an itinerary makes it easier to combine the understanding of faith with professional commitment and Christian action. Apart from their theological formation, educators need also to cultivate their spiritual formation in order to develop their relationship with Jesus Christ and become a Master like Him. In this sense, the formational journey of both lay and consecrated educators must be combined with the moulding of the person towards greater conformity with Christ (cf. *Rm* 8:29) and of the educational community around Christ the Master. Moreover, the Catholic school is well aware that the community that it forms must be constantly nourished and compared with the sources from which the reason for its existence derives: the saving word of God in Sacred Scripture, in Tradition, above all liturgical and sacramental Tradition, enlightened by the Magisterium of the Church.[28]

The contribution of consecrated persons to shared formation

27. Consecrated persons who profess the evangelical counsels show that they live for God and of God and become concrete witnesses to the Trinitarian love, so that people can experience the charm of divine beauty. Thus, the first and foremost contribution to the shared mission is the evangelical deep-rootedness of the

---

[26] *Ibid.*

[27] Cf. Sacred Congregation for Catholic Education, *Lay Catholics in Schools: Witnesses to Faith*, no. 60.

[28] Cf. Vatican Council II, Dogmatic Constitution on Divine Revelation *Dei Verbum* (18th November 1965), no. 10: *AAS* 58 (1966), 822.

lives of consecrated persons. Because of their vocational journey, they possess a theological-spiritual preparation that, centred on the mystery of Christ living in the Church, needs to unceasingly progress in step with the Church that progresses in history towards the "complete truth" (*Jn* 16:13). Again within this exquisitely ecclesial dynamic, consecrated persons also are invited to share the fruits of their formation with the laity, especially with those who feel that they are called "[to share] specific aspects and moments of the spirituality and mission of the Institute".[29] In this way, Institutes of consecrated life and Societies of apostolic life involved in education will manage to assure an essential openness to the Church and keep alive the spirit of the Founders and Foundresses, while also renewing a particularly precious aspect of the tradition of the Catholic school. From the very beginning, in fact, Founders and Foundresses paid special attention to the *formation of the educators* and they often devoted their best energies to this. Such formation, then as now, is not only aimed at strengthening professional skills, but above all, at highlighting the vocational dimension of the teaching profession, promoting the development of a mentality that is inspired by evangelical values, according to the specific characteristics of the Institute's mission. Therefore, "formation programmes which include regular courses of study and prayerful reflection on the founder, the charism and the constitutions of the institute are particularly beneficial".[30]

28. In many religious Institutes, sharing the educational mission with the laity has already existed for some time, having been born with the religious community present in the school. The development of "spiritual families", of groups of "associated lay people" or other forms that permit the lay faithful to draw spiritual and apostolic fruitfulness from the original charism, appears as a positive element and one of great hope for the future of the Catholic educational mission.

---

[29] Congregation for Institutes of Consecrated Life and Societies of Apostolic Life, *Starting Afresh from Christ,* no. 31.

[30] Congregation for Institutes of Consecrated Life and Societies of Apostolic Life. *Fraternal Life in Community,* (2nd February 1994), no. 45.

29. It is almost superfluous to note that, within the perspective of the Church-communion, these programmes of formation for sharing in the mission and lives of the laity, in the light of the relative charism, should be designed and implemented even where vocations to the consecrated life are numerous.

The contribution of lay persons to shared formation

30. While invited to deepen their vocation as educators in the Catholic school in communion with consecrated persons, the lay faithful also are called in the common formational journey to give the original and irreplaceable contribution of their full ecclesial subjectivity. This involves, first and foremost, that they discover and live in their "life of a lay person […] a specific "wonderful" vocation within the Church":[31] the vocation to "seek the kingdom of God by engaging in temporal affairs and directing them according to God's will".[32] As educators they are called on to live "in faith a secular vocation in the communitarian structure of the school: with the best possible professional qualifications, with an apostolic intention inspired by faith, for the integral formation of the human person".[33]

31. It should be emphasised that the special contribution that lay educators can bring to the formational journey derives precisely from their secular nature that makes them especially able to grasp "the signs of the times".[34] In fact, by living their faith in the everyday conditions of their families and society, they can help the entire educational community to distinguish more precisely the evangelical values and the opposite values that these signs contain.

32. With the gradual development of their ecclesial vocation, lay people become increasingly more aware of their participation in the educational mission of the Church. At the same time, they are also driven to carry out an active role in the spiritual animation of the

---

[31] Sacred Congregation for Catholic Education, *Lay Catholics in Schools: Witnesses to Faith*, no. 7.

[32] Vatican Council II, Dogmatic Constitution on the Church *Lumen gentium* (21st November 1964), n. 31: *AAS* 57 (1965), 37.

[33] Sacred Congregation for Catholic Education, *Lay Catholics in Schools: Witnesses to Faith*, no. 24.

[34] Vatican Council II, Pastoral Constitution on the Church in the Modern World *Gaudium et spes*, n. 4: *AAS* 58 (1966), 1027.

community that they build together with the consecrated persons. "Communion and mutuality in the Church are never one way streets".[35] If, in fact, in the past it was mostly priests and religious who spiritually nourished and directed the lay faithful, now it is often "the lay faithful themselves [who] can and should help priests and religious in the course of their spiritual and pastoral journey".[36]

33. In the perspective of formation, by sharing their life of prayer and opportune forms of community life, the lay faithful and consecrated persons will nourish their reflection, their sense of fraternity and generous dedication. In this common catechetical-theological and spiritual formational journey, we can see the face of a Church that presents that of Christ, praying, listening, learning and teaching in fraternal communion.

Formation in the spirit of communion for educating

34. By its very nature, the Catholic school requires the presence and involvement of educators that are not only culturally and spiritually formed, but also intentionally directed at developing their community educational commitment in an authentic spirit of ecclesial communion.

35. It is also through their formational journey that educators are called on to build relationships at professional, personal and spiritual levels, according to the logic of communion. For each one this involves being open, welcoming, disposed to a deep exchange of ideas, convivial and living a fraternal life within the educational community itself. The parable of the talents (*Mt* 25:14-30) helps us to understand how each one is called to make his or her gifts bear fruit and to welcome the riches of others within the shared educational mission.

36. The shared mission, besides, is enriched by the differences that the lay faithful and consecrated persons bring when they come together in different expressions of charism. These charisms are

---

[35] Congregation for Institutes of Consecrated Life and Societies of Apostolic Life, *Starting Afresh from Christ*, no. 31

[36] John Paul II, Post-synodal Apostolic Exhortation *Christifideles laici*, no. 61: *AAS* 81 (1989), 514.

none other than different gifts with which the same Spirit enriches the Church and the world.[37] In the Catholic school, therefore, "by avoiding both confrontation and homologation, the reciprocity of vocations seems to be a particularly fertile prospect for enriching the ecclesial value of educational communities. In them the various vocations […] are correlative, different and mutual paths that converge to bring to fulfilment the charism of charisms: love".[38]

37. Organised according to the diversities of persons and vocations, but vivified by the same spirit of communion, the educational community of the Catholic school aims at creating increasingly deeper relationships of communion that are in themselves educational. Precisely in this, it "expresses the variety and beauty of the various vocations and the fruitfulness at educational and pedagogical levels that this contributes to the life of the school".[39]

Witness and culture of communion

38. This fruitfulness is expressed, above all, in the witness offered by the educational community. Certainly in schools, education is essentially accomplished through teaching, which is the vehicle through which ideas and beliefs are communicated. In this sense, "words are the main roads in educating the mind".[40] This does not mean, however, that education is not accomplished in other situations of scholastic life. Thus teachers, just like every person who lives and works in a scholastic environment, educate, or they can also dis-educate, with their verbal and non-verbal behaviour. "The central figure in the work of educating, and especially in education in the faith, which is the summit of the person's formation and is his or her most appropriate horizon, is specifically the form of witness".[41] "More than ever this demands

---

[37] Cf. Congregation for Institutes of Consecrated Life and Societies of Apostolic Life. *Fraternal Life in Community* (2nd February 1994), no. 45.

[38] Congregation for Catholic Education, *Consecrated Persons and their Mission in Schools*, no. 21.

[39] *Ibid.*, n. 43.

[40] Benedict XVI, Speech to the Representatives of some Muslim Communities (20th August 2005): *AAS* 97 (2005), 918.

[41] Benedict XVI, Address to Rome's Ecclesial Diocesan Convention on the Family and Christian Community (6th June 2005): *AAS* 97 (2005), 815.

that witness, nourished by prayer, be the all-encompassing milieu of every Catholic school. Teachers, as witnesses, account for the hope that nourishes their own lives (cf. 1 *Pt* 3:15) by living the truth they propose to their pupils, always in reference to the one they have encountered and whose dependable goodness they have sampled with joy. And so with Saint Augustine they say: "We who speak and you who listen acknowledge ourselves as fellow disciples of a single teacher" (*Sermons*, 23:2)".[42] In educational communities, therefore, the style of life has great influence, especially if the consecrated persons and the lay faithful work together, fully sharing the commitment to develop, in the school, "an atmosphere animated by a spirit of liberty and charity based on the Gospel".[43] This requires that each one contributes the specific gift of his or her vocation to construct a family supported by charity and by the spirit of the beatitudes.

39. By giving witness of communion, the Catholic educational community is able to *educate for communion*, which, as a gift that comes from above, animates the project of formation for living together in harmony and being welcoming. Not only does it cultivate in the students the cultural values that derive from the Christian vision of reality, but it also involves each one of them in the life of the community, where values are mediated by authentic interpersonal relationships among the various members that form it, and by the individual and community acceptance of them. In this way, the life of communion of the educational community assumes the value of an educational principle, of a paradigm that directs its formational action as a service for the achievement of a culture of communion. Education in the Catholic school, therefore, through the tools of teaching and learning, "is not given for the purpose of gaining power but as an aid towards a fuller understanding of, and communion with man, events and things".[44] This principle affects every scholastic

---

[42] Benedict XVI, Speech to the Bishops of Ontario, Canada, on their *ad limina Apostolorum* Visit (8th September 2006): *L'Osservatore Romano* (9th September 2006), 9.

[43] Vatican Council II, Declaration on Christian Education *Gravissimum educationis*, no. 8: *AAS* 58 (1966), 734.

[44] Sacred Congregation for Catholic Education, *The Catholic School*, no. 56.

activity, the teaching and even all the after-school activities such as sport, theatre and commitment in social work, which promote the creative contribution of the students and their socialisation.

Educational community and vocational pastoral activity

40. The shared mission experienced by an educational community of lay and consecrated persons, with an active vocational conscience, makes the Catholic school a pedagogical place that favours *vocational pastoral activity*. The very composition of such an educational community of a Catholic school highlights the diversity and complementarity of vocations in the Church,[45] of which it, too, is an expression. In this sense, the communitarian dynamics of the formational experience become the horizon where the student can feel what it means to be a member of the biggest community which is the Church. And to experience the Church means to personally meet the living Christ in it: "a young man can truly understand Christ's will and his own vocation only to the extent that he has a personal experience of Christ".[46] In this sense, the Catholic school is committed to guiding its students to knowing themselves, their attitudes and their interior resources, educating them in spending their lives responsibly as a daily response to God's call. Thus, the Catholic school accompanies its students in conscious choices of life: to follow their vocation to the priesthood or to consecrated life or to accomplish their Christian vocation in family, professional and social life.

41. In fact, the daily dialogue and confrontation with lay and consecrated educators, who offer a joyful witness of their calling, will more easily direct a young person in formation to consider his or her life as a vocation, as a journey to be lived together, grasping the signs through which God leads to the fullness of existence. Similarly, it will make him or her understand how necessary it is to know how to listen, to interiorise values, to learn to assume commitments and make life choices.

---

[45] Cf. John Paul II, Post-synodal Apostolic Exhortation *Christifideles laici*, no. 20: *AAS* 81 (1989), 425.

[46] Benedict XVI, Address to Seminarians (19th August 2005): *AAS* 97 (2005), 880.

42. Therefore, the formational experience of the Catholic school constitutes an impressive barrier against the influence of a widespread mentality that leads young people especially "to consider themselves and their lives as a series of sensations to be experienced rather than as a work to be accomplished".[47] At the same time, it contributes to insuring strong character formation [....] capable both of resisting the debilitating influence of relativism and of living up to the demands made on them by their Baptism".[48]

[47] John Paul II, Encyclical Letter *Centesimus annus* (1st May 1991), n. 39: *AAS* 83 (1991), 842.

[48] Sacred Congregation for Catholic Education, *The Catholic School*, no. 12.

III. COMMUNION FOR
OPENING ONESELF TOWARDS OTHERS

43. The communion lived by the educators of the Catholic school contributes to making the entire educational sphere a place of communion open to external reality and not just closed in on itself. *Educating in communion* and *for communion* means directing students to grow authentically as persons who "gradually learn to open themselves up to life as it is, and to create in themselves a definite attitude to life"[49] that will help them to open their views and their hearts to the world that surrounds them, able to see things critically, with a sense of responsibility and a desire for a constructive commitment. Two orders of motivation, anthropological and theological, form the basis of this opening towards the world.

Anthropological and theological foundations

44. The human being, as a person, is a unity of soul and body that is dynamically realised through its opening to a relation with others. A person is formed for *being-with* and *for others,* which is realised in love. Now, it is precisely love that drives a person to gradually broaden the range of his or her relations beyond the sphere of private life and family affections, to assume the range of universality and to embrace – at least by desire – all mankind. This same drive also contains a strong formational requirement: the requirement to learn to read the interdependence of a world that is increasingly besieged by the same problems of a global nature, as a strong ethical sign for the people of our time; like a call to emerge from that vision of man that tends to see each one as an isolated individual. It is the requirement to form man as a person: a subject that in love builds his historical, cultural, spiritual and religious identity, placing it in dialogue with other persons, in a constant exchange of gifts offered and received. Within the context of globalisation, people must be formed in

---

[49] *Ibid.*, no. 31.

22

such a way as to respect the identity, culture, history, religion and especially the suffering and needs of others, conscious that "we are all really responsible for all".[50]

45. This requirement assumes even more importance and urgency within the sphere of the Catholic *faith*, experienced in the *love* of ecclesial *communion*. In fact, the Church, the place of communion and image of Trinitarian love, "is alive with the love enkindled by the Spirit of Christ".[51] The Spirit acts as an "interior power" that harmonises the hearts of believers with Christ's heart and "transforms the heart of the ecclesial community, so that it becomes a witness before the world to the love of the Father".[52] Thus, "beginning with intra-ecclesial communion, charity of its nature opens out into a service that is universal; it inspires in us a *commitment to practical and concrete love for every human being*".[53] In this sense, the Church is not an end in itself, it exists to show God to the world; it exists for others.

46. In the same way, inasmuch as it is an ecclesial subject, the Catholic school acts as the Christian ferment of the world. In it, students learn to overcome individualism and to discover, in the light of faith, that they are called to live responsibly a specific vocation to friendship with Christ and in solidarity with other persons. Basically, the school is called to be a living witness of the love of God among us. It can, moreover, become a means through which it is possible to discern, in the light of the Gospel, what is positive in the world, what needs to be transformed and what injustices must be overcome. A vigilant acceptance of the contributions of the world to the life of the school also nourishes and promotes open communion, especially in some educational environments, such as education to peace, to living together, to justice and to brotherhood.

---

[50] John Paul II, Encyclical Letter *Sollicitudo rei socialis* (30th December 1987), no. 38: *AAS* 80 (1988), 566.

[51] Benedict XVI, Encyclical Letter *Deus caritas est*, no. 28b: *AAS* 98 (2006), 240.

[52] *Ibid.*, no. 19: 233.

[53] John Paul II, Apostolic Letter *Novo millennio ineunte*, no. 49: *AAS* 93 (2001), 302.

Builders of open communion

47. Sharing the same educational mission with a diversity of persons, vocations and states of life is undoubtedly a strong point of the Catholic school in its participation in the missionary life of the Church, in the opening of ecclesial communion towards the world. In this respect, a first precious contribution comes from communion between lay and consecrated faithful in the school.

Lay persons who, because of their family and social relationships, live immersed in the world, can promote the opening of the educational community to a constructive relationship with cultural, civil and political institutions, with various social groups – from the most informal ones to those most organised – present in the territory. The Catholic school also assures its presence in the locality through its active cooperation with other educational institutions, especially with Catholic centres for higher studies, with which they share a special ecclesial bond, and with local bodies and various social agencies. In this sphere, faithful to its inspiration, it contributes to building a network of relationships that helps students to develop their sense of belonging, and society itself to develop a sense of solidarity.

Consecrated persons also participate, as "true signs of Christ in the world",[54] in this opening to the outside world by sharing the gifts they bear. They must demonstrate especially that religious consecration has much to say to every culture in that it helps to reveal the truth of the human being. The witness of their evangelical life must reveal that "holiness is the highest humanising proposal of man and of history; it is a project that everyone on earth can make his or her own".[55]

48. Another pillar of *open communion* is formed by the relationship between the Catholic school and the families that choose it for the education of their children. This relationship appears as full participation of the parents in the life of the educational community, not only because of their primary responsibility in the education of

---

[54] John Paul II, Post-synodal Apostolic Exhortation *Vita consecrata*, no. 25: *AAS* 88 (1996), 398.

[55] Congregation for Catholic Education, *Consecrated Persons and their Mission in Schools*, no. 12.

their children, but also by virtue of their sharing in the identity and project that characterise the Catholic school and which they must know and share with a readiness that comes from within. It is precisely because of this that the educational community identifies the decisive space for cooperation between school and family in the *educational project*, to be made known and implemented with a spirit of communion, through the contribution of everyone, discerning responsibilities, roles and competences. Parents in particular are required to enrich the communion around this project, making the family climate that must characterise the educating community more alive and explicit. For this reason, in willingly welcoming parents' cooperation, Catholic schools consider essential to their mission the service of *permanent formation offered to families*, to support them in their educating task and to develop an increasingly closer bond between the values proposed by the school and those proposed by the family.

49. The Christian-inspired associations and groups that unite the parents of Catholic schools represent a further bridge between the educational community and the world that surrounds it. These associations and groups can strengthen the bond of reciprocity between school and society, maintaining the educational community open to the wider social community and, at the same time, creating an awareness in society and its institutions of the presence and action carried out by Catholic schools in the territory.

50. At an ecclesial level also, the communion experienced within the Catholic school can and must be open to an enriching exchange in a more extensive communion with the parish, the diocese, ecclesial movements and the universal Church. This means that lay persons (educators and parents) and consecrated persons belonging to the educational community must take a meaningful part, even outside the walls of the Catholic school, in the life of the local Church. The members of the diocesan clergy and the lay persons of the local Christian community, who do not always have an adequate knowledge of the Catholic school, must discover it as a *school of the Christian community*, a living expression of the same Church of Christ to which they belong.

51. If lived authentically and profoundly, the ecclesial dimension of the educational community of the Catholic school cannot be limited to a relationship with the local Christian community. Almost by natural extension, it tends to open onto the horizons of the universal Church. In this sense, the international dimension of many religious families offers consecrated persons the enrichment of communion with those who share the same mission in various parts of the world. At the same time, it offers a witness to the living strength of a charism that unites, over and above all, differences. The richness of this communion in the universal Church can and must be shared, for example, through regional or world level formational occasions and meetings. These should also involve lay persons (educators and parents) who, because of their state of life, share the educational mission of the relative charisms.

52. Structured in this way, the Catholic school appears as an educational community in which ecclesial and missionary communion develops in depth and grows in breadth. A communion can be experienced in it that becomes an effective witness to the presence of Christ alive in the educational community gathered together in His name (cf. *Mt* 18:20) and that, precisely for this reason, opens to a deeper understanding of reality and a more convinced commitment to renewal of the world. In fact, "if we think and live by virtue of communion with Christ, then our eyes will be opened",[56] and we will understand that "real revolution, the decisive change in the world, comes from God".[57]

53. The communion experienced in the educational community, animated and sustained by lay and consecrated persons joined together in the same mission, makes the Catholic school a community environment filled with the spirit of the Gospel. Now, this community environment appears as a privileged place for the formation of young people in the construction of a world based on dialogue and the search for communion, rather than in

---

[56] Benedict XVI, Homily during the Eucharistic Celebration in Marienfeld (21st August 2005): *AAS* 97 (2005), 892.

[57] Benedict XVI, Homily at the Prayer Vigil in Marienfeld (20th August 2005): *AAS* 97 (2005), 885.

contrast; on the mutual acceptance of differences rather than on their opposition. In this way, with its educational project taking inspiration from ecclesial communion and the civilisation of love, the Catholic school can contribute considerably to illuminating the minds of many, so that "there will arise a generation of new persons, the moulders of a new humanity".[58]

---

[58] Vatican Council II, Pastoral Constitution on the Church in the Modern World *Gaudium et spes*, no. 30: *AAS* 58 (1966), 1050.

Conclusion

54. "In a world where cultural challenge is the first, the most provocative and the most effect-bearing",[59] the Catholic school is well aware of the onerous commitments it is called to face and it preserves its utmost importance even in present circumstances.

55. When it is animated by lay and consecrated persons that live the same educational mission in sincere unity, the Catholic school shows the face of a community that tends towards an increasingly deeper communion. This communion knows how to be welcoming with regard to people as they mature, making them feel, through the maternal solicitude of the Church, that God carries the life of each son and daughter of His in His heart. It knows how to involve young people in a global formation experience, to direct and accompany, in the light of the Good News, their search for meaning, even in unusual and often tortuous forms, but with an alarming urgency. A communion, finally, that inasmuch as it is based on Christ, acknowledges Him and announces Him to each and everyone as the only true Master (cf. *Mt* 23:8).

56. In presenting this document to those who live the educational mission in the Church, we entrust all Catholic schools to the Virgin Mary, Mother and educator of Christ and of persons, so that, like the servants at the wedding of Cana, they may humbly follow her loving invitation: "Do whatever He tells you" (*Jn* 2:5) and may they, thus, be together with the whole Church, "the home and the school of communion"[60] for the men and women of our time.

The Holy Father, during the Audience granted to the undersigned Prefect, approved this document and authorised its publication.
Rome, 8th September 2007, Feast of the Nativity of the Blessed Virgin Mary.

Zenon Card. Grocholewski, *Prefect*
Msgr. Angelo Vincenzo Zani, *Undersecretary*

---

[59] John Paul II, Speech to Parents, Students and Teachers of Catholic Schools (23rd November 1991), n. 6: *AAS* 84 (1992), 1136.

[60] John Paul II, Apostolic Letter *Novo millennio ineunte*, n. 43: *AAS* 93 (2001), 296.